Lorde

by **Sarah Tieck**

Big Buddy Books
An Imprint of Abdo Publishing
www.abdopublishing.com

www.abdopublishing.com

Published by Abdo Publishing, a division of ABDO, PO Box 398166, Minneapolis, Minnesota 55439.
Copyright © 2015 by Abdo Consulting Group, Inc. International copyrights reserved in all countries. No part
of this book may be reproduced in any form without written permission from the publisher. Big Buddy Books™
is a trademark and logo of Abdo Publishing.

Printed in the United States of America, North Mankato, Minnesota.
092014
012015

Cover Photo: ASSOCIATED PRESS.
Interior Photos: ASSOCIATED PRESS (pp. 11, 28); Getty Images (pp. 20, 23, 27); Paul A. Hebert/Invision/AP (p. 13);
    ©iStockphoto.com (p. 9); Frank Micelotta/Invision/AP (p. 17); Chris Pizzello/Invision/AP (p. 29); RTNKabik/
    MediaPunch/IPx (p. 5); Joel Ryan/Invision/AP (p. 14); Matt Sayles/Invision/AP (p. 19); Shutterstock.com (p. 25);
    Owen Sweeney/Invision/AP (p. 11); WireImage (pp. 7, 8).

Coordinating Series Editor: Rochelle Baltzer
Contributing Editors: Megan M. Gunderson, Marcia Zappa
Graphic Design: Maria Hosley

Library of Congress Cataloging-in-Publication Data

Tieck, Sarah, 1976-
  Lorde : singing sensation / Sarah Tieck.
     pages cm. -- (Big buddy biographies)
  Audience: 7-11.
  ISBN 978-1-62403-569-2
  1. Lorde, 1996---Juvenile literature. 2. Singers--New Zealand--Biography--Juvenile literature. I. Title.
  ML3930.L67T54 2015
  782.42164092--dc23
  [B]
                              2014026438

Contents

> Lorde is known for her soulful, unusual voice.

Singing Star

Lorde is a talented singer and songwriter. She has won awards for her music. Fans around the world love Lorde's songs.

AUSTRALIA

TASMAN

SEA

Takapuna

Auckland

NEW ZEALAND

N W E S

Family Ties

Lorde's real name is Ella Marija Lani Yelich-O'Connor. She was born in Takapuna, New Zealand, on November 7, 1996. Takapuna is near the city of Auckland.

Ella's parents are Sonja Yelich and Vic O'Connor. Ella's older sister is Jerry. Her younger brother is Angelo, and her younger sister is India.

Lorde attended the 2014 Grammy Awards with her parents.

Lorde's mom is a poet. She encouraged her daughter to read. Lorde believes this helped her write songs later on.

Starting Out

As a child, Ella enjoyed writing. She wrote **fictional** stories. Young Ella also liked to sing. Around age 13, she wrote her first song.

Ella was interested in royalty and the very rich. So when she began **performing** her music, she took the stage name "Lorde." The idea came from a type of ruler called a lord. She added the e to make it more **feminine**.

Lorde grew up in Takapuna. This is a beach town on New Zealand's North Island.

Words and Ideas

Lorde started out writing short **fiction**. She liked sharing her feelings and ideas. As she started writing songs, she quickly came to love music.

Lorde's sound and style is different from most teen **pop** singers. Books and other **performers** have **influenced** her work. They have given her new ideas.

Author T.S. Eliot (*left*) is one of Lorde's influences. She is also interested in rappers Drake (*right*) and Kanye West (*below*).

Big Break

In 2013, Lorde released an extended play (EP) called *The Love Club*. EPs have more than one song but are not long enough to be an album. "Bravado," "Royals," and "Biting Down" were some of the songs on Lorde's EP.

Lorde writes songs about her life. But, she works to make her music sound new and different.

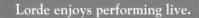

At first, Lorde's EP could be downloaded for free. Soon, about 60,000 people around the world had downloaded *The Love Club*. This caught the attention of a record company in the United States. It worked with Lorde to sell her music.

"Royals" made Lorde the first solo artist from New Zealand to have a number one hit in the United States.

First Album

After Lorde's successful EP, her fans were excited for more music! In 2013, she put out the full-length album *Pure Heroine*. "Royals" and "Tennis Court" were hit songs from that album. "Team" was also popular.

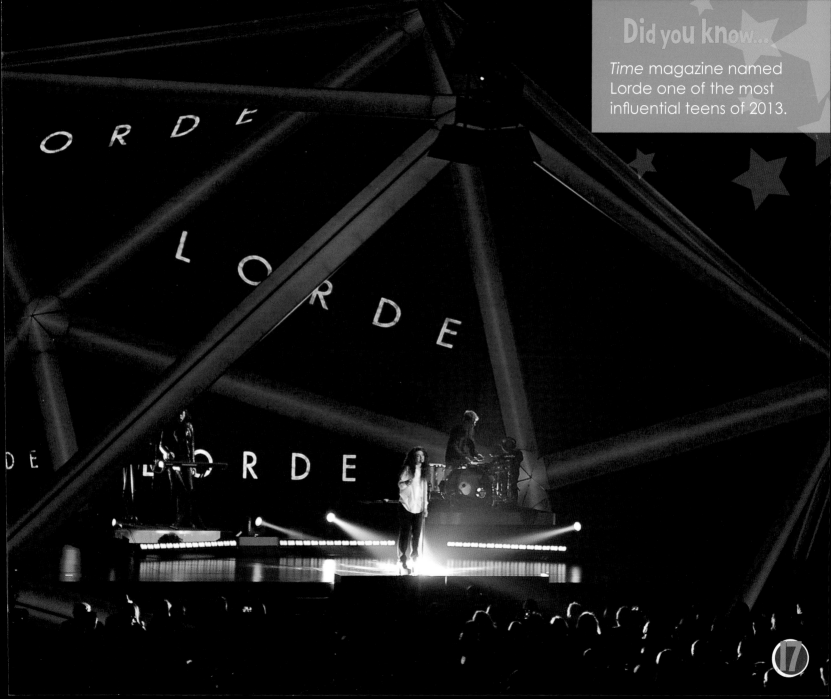

Award Winner

Soon, Lorde was recognized for her singing and songwriting. In 2014, she won two **Grammy Awards**. They were Best **Pop** Solo **Performance** and Song of the Year for "Royals."

Lorde wrote "Royals" with Joel Little.

Since her music has grown more popular, Lorde performs for more and more people.

A Singer's Life

As a singer and songwriter, Lorde spends time working on her songs. She goes to recording **studios** to make albums. She plans and practices live **performances** for fans around the world.

21

Lorde is known for being quiet and private. Still, she must **promote** her albums. So, she appears on television and in magazines. She talks about her music and style.

Lorde has done interviews on the radio to promote her music.

Off the Stage

Lorde spends free time with her
family and friends in New Zealand.
She enjoys cooking. She also likes to
read short fiction.

Lorde grew up close to a beach. She enjoys spending time in and near water.

Lorde likes to help others when she can. In 2014, a Muppet was made to look like her. It was sold to make money for the Starship Foundation. This group helps raise money for children's health care.

Lorde supports equality for women. She uses her fame to help make others more aware of issues.

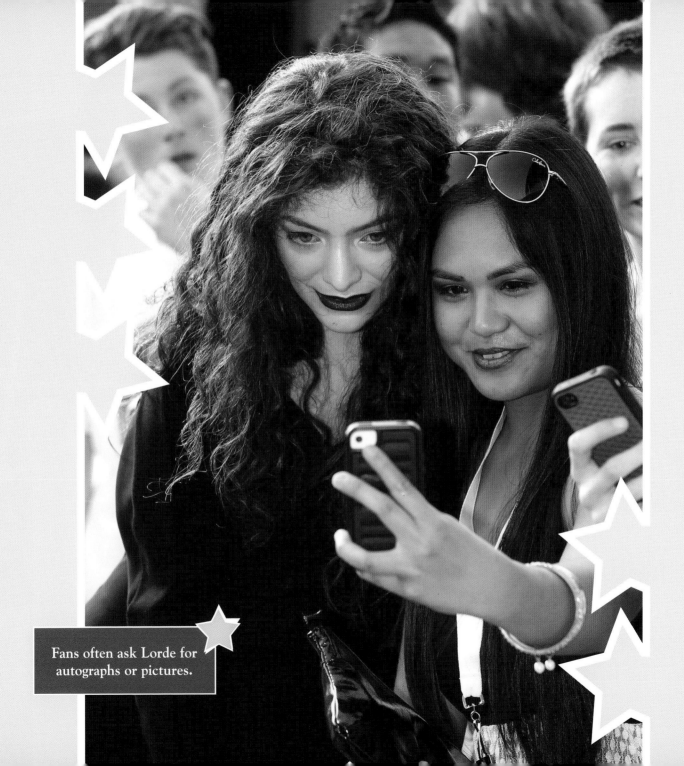

Fans often ask Lorde for autographs or pictures.

Famous rocker David Bowie says he is excited for performers like Lorde. He thinks they will make a strong future for music.

Buzz

Many people are excited about Lorde's music. In 2014, Lorde **headlined** a tour. She **performed** live around the world. Fans look forward to more songs from Lorde!

In 2014, Lorde won the award for Top New Artist at the Billboard Music Awards.

Snapshot

★**Name**: Ella Marija Lani Yelich-O'Connor

★**Birthday**: November 7, 1996

★**Birthplace**: Takapuna, New Zealand

★**EP**: *The Love Club*

★**Album**: *Pure Heroine*

Important Words

feminine (FEH-muh-nuhn) of, relating to, or suited to women or girls.

fiction stories that are not real.

Grammy Award any of the awards given each year by the National Academy of Recording Arts and Sciences. Grammy Awards honor the year's best accomplishments in music.

headline to be the main act in a show.

influence to have an effect on something without the direct use of force.

perform to do something in front of an audience. A performance is the act of doing something, such as singing or acting, in front of an audience. A performer is someone who performs.

pop relating to popular music.

promote to help something become known.

release to make available to the public.

studio a place where music is recorded.

Websites

To learn more about Big Buddy Biographies, visit **booklinks.abdopublishing.com**. These links are routinely monitored and updated to provide the most current information available.

Index